Mrs. Norsworthy

Mathematics Games
for Fun and Practice

Alan Barson

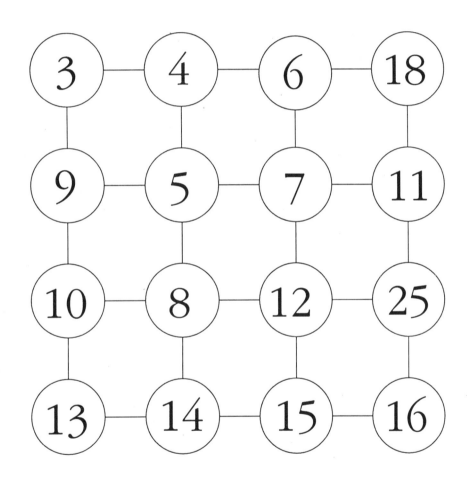

Addison-Wesley Publishing Company

Menlo Park, California • Reading, Massachusetts • New York
Don Mills, Ontario • Wokingham, England • Amsterdam • Bonn
Sydney • Singapore • Tokyo • Madrid • San Juan • Paris
Seoul, Korea • Milan • Mexico City • Taipei, Taiwan

P9-BJP-895

This book is published by Innovative Learning Publications, an imprint of Addison-Wesley Publishing Company

The blackline masters that accompany this publication are designed to be used with appropriate duplicating equipment to reproduce copies for classroom use. Addison-Wesley Publishing Company grants permission to classroom teachers to reproduce these masters.

Copyright © 1992 by Addison-Wesley Publishing Company, Inc.
All rights reserved. Printed in the United States of America.

ISBN 0-201-29106-1
6 7 8 9 10-ML-95

Contents

Introduction

Because games are enjoyable and provide thoughtful moments of logic, fun, and skill, they are a powerful means of improving mathematics skills. To be most effective, games should be structured so that they are neither all skill nor all luck. Ideally, they should combine skill with a touch of luck. It is also important that the setting of the game be familiar. Games that are similar to tic-tac-toe, checkers, and bingo, for example, provide students with a familiar framework and make the playing of the game much more interesting.

The games in *Mathematics Games for Fun and Practice* were developed with these points in mind. In addition, the games were constructed so that one specific skill is emphasized, even though other skills may play a secondary role. A game that stresses too many concepts will not foster growth in the skill area to be reinforced, remediated, or enriched. The strategy games in this book also help students develop their logical thinking and problem-solving skills. These activities are motivational and tend to improve students' attitudes toward mathematics and problem solving.

The 38 games in *Mathematics Games for Fun and Practice* are designed for Grades 4–8 and are grouped according to the following major concepts:
- Computation
- Geometry
- Measurement
- Fractions, decimals, and percent
- Properties of numbers
- Problem solving

Most games will be played for five to ten minutes. If there is time in the period, students can repeat a game. Your role should be that of facilitator, clarifying the directions if needed, monitoring the progress of the students, and providing students with a means of recording their scores and tracking their progress. In some cases, you may wish to make transparencies for the overhead projector to introduce a game or to play a game with the entire class. You may also need to act as arbitrator on occasion when there is disagreement between students about a correct answer or an acceptable move on the playing board.

After students become familiar with the games, you may wish to hold a tournament. The blank form on page vi provides a convenient way to set up a tournament and keep track of players and winners. It is designed for 16 players. The players' names should be written on the vertical lines on the bottom tier of the chart. If you wish to

Tournament Form

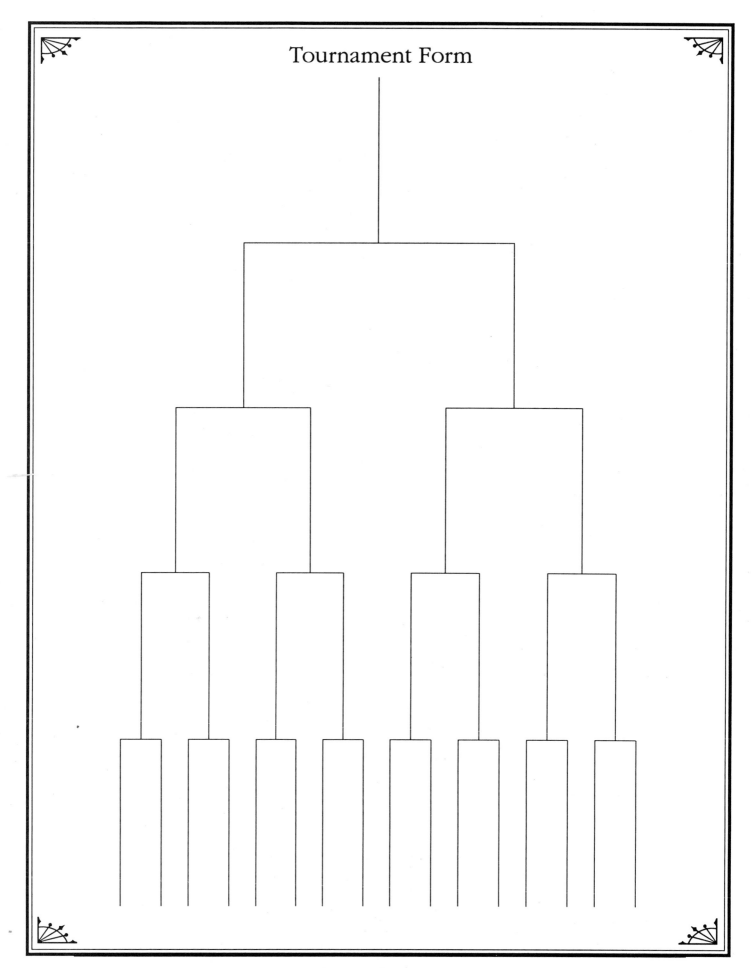

have a tournament for 32 players, make two copies of the chart, connect the top line on each sheet with a horizontal line, and add one more vertical line for the final winner. If you have an odd number of students playing in a tournament, have one student join after the first round and record his or her name on the second tier of the chart.

Directions and Suggestions

This book contains 38 playing board designs and sets of directions. In order to gain the fullest benefit from these games, the following steps should be considered before using the playing boards with students:

1. Photocopy each playing board and set of directions and paste them on posterboard for durability. If your copier enlarges, you may want to make larger playing boards.
2. Color the playing boards with colored markers or crayons to make them more attractive. (Students could also do this.)
3. Laminate the boards and the directions to keep them clean and durable. Clear contact paper can also be used for this purpose.
4. Put each playing board, directions, and materials needed to play the game in a box or a large self-lock plastic bag. Then, when students want to play a game, they can just take the container and begin the game.

You will need three basic items for the games:*
- dice
- different colored disks or counters (preferably transparent)
- blank wooden cubes (preferably 1-inch)

To label the wooden cubes, you can write the information directly on the cubes with permanent ink or you can use gummed labels. You can also photocopy the labels from the directions sheet and tape them onto the cubes.

When you've completed the task of making the game packets, you will have 38 games. I hope you enjoy the games and find them useful.

A.H. Barson

*These materials can be purchased from Dale Seymour Publications or Cuisenaire. For a catalog or further information, call:

Dale Seymour Publications   1 800 USA-1100
Cuisenaire   1 800 237-3142

Mathematics Games
for Fun and Practice

Plus Game

	A	B	C	D	E	F
U	0	+1	+2	+3	+4	+5
V	-1	0	+1	+2	+3	+4
W	-2	-1	0	+1	+2	+3
X	-3	-2	-1	0	+1	+2
Y	-4	-3	-2	-1	0	+1
Z	-5	-4	-3	-2	-1	0

Plus Game

Players
Two players

Materials
1 die and 2 cubes
Label one cube with the following faces:

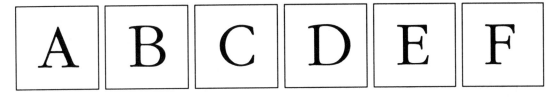

Label the second cube with the following faces:

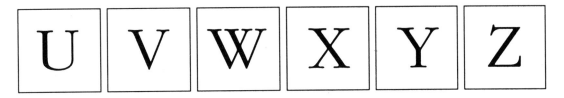

Object
To get the highest total for 10 rounds

To Start
Choose the starting player by rolling the die. The player with the higher number goes first.

Rules
1. The starting player rolls both cubes and finds the number on the chart that represents the intersection of the two letters rolled.
2. The player writes that number down on paper.
3. Players keep a running total of their numbers.
4. Players alternate turns.
5. The player with the highest total after 10 rolls wins.

Make a Square

5	1	-2	-3	0
36	24	10	4	2
16	9	25	3	8
3	6	7	12	9
11	30	20	15	18

Make a Square

Players
Two players

Materials
10 red disks, 10 blue disks, and a pair of dice

Object
To form a square with four disks

To Start
Choose the starting player by rolling the dice. The player with the higher number goes first.

Rules
1. Players alternate turns rolling the dice.
2. The starting player adds, subtracts, multiplies, or divides the two numbers rolled to get a number on the board. He or she then places a disk on that number.
3. The first player to cover four points that form a square wins. For example:

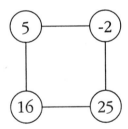
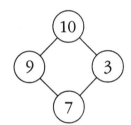

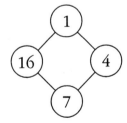
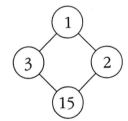

Playing with Numbers

20	1	16	2
40	4	36	18
$7\frac{1}{2}$	25	9	$1\frac{1}{2}$
12	3	$4\frac{1}{2}$	0
10	30	8	6

Playing with Numbers

Players

Two players

Materials

10 red disks, 10 blue disks, 1 die, and 1 cube
Label the cube with the following faces:

square	times two	square minus number	multiple	half of 3 times number	any even number

Object

To get three disks in a row—vertically, horizontally, or diagonally

To Start

Choose the starting player by rolling the die. The player with the higher number goes first.

Rules

1. The starting player rolls the die and the cube. He or she performs the direction on the cube with the roll on the die. For example:

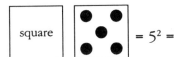 $= 5^2 = 25$ 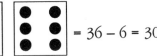 $= 36 - 6 = 30$

2. The player covers the answer with a disk. If there is more than one answer, only one answer can be covered. For example:

  can cover 3, 6, 9, 12, etc.

3. Players alternate turns.
4. The first player to cover three in a row wins.
5. If the cube comes up with "any even number" and the die is an even number, the player can choose any even number on the board. If the die is an odd number, the player loses his or her turn.
6. The first player to get three disks in a row wins.

Division Lineup

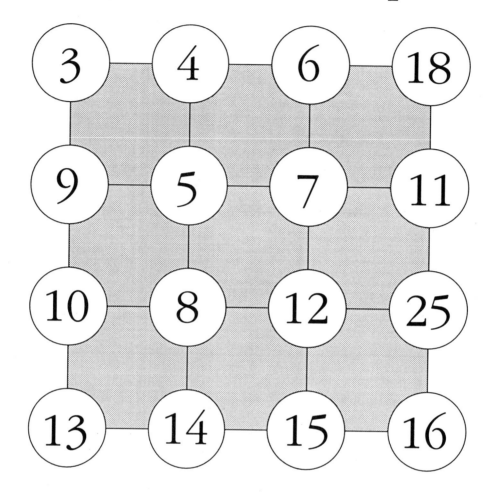

18   108   630   51   500   540
162   20   16
169   9   132   240
1260   972
135   210   180   272   13
102
12   152   196   320
17   54   144   14
90   27
182   19   80   5
68   714

Division Lineup

Players

Two players

Materials

8 red disks, 8 blue disks, and 1 die

Object

To get three disks in a row—vertically, horizontally, or diagonally

To Start

Choose the starting player by rolling the die. The player with the higher number goes first.

Rules

1. On any turn, a player uses any two numbers from the bottom box and divides them. If the answer is on the playing board, the player covers it with a disk.
2. Players alternate turns.
3. The first player to get three disks in a row wins.

Variation: A number from the bottom box may be used only once.

North by Northwest

N
↑

8	3	5	5	3
2	9	7	2	1
1	0	**Start Here**	7	6
3	2	2	4	5
6	4	8	1	8
5	1	6	3	10

North by Northwest

Players
Two players

Materials
1 red disk, 1 blue disk, 1 die, and 3 cubes
Label one cube with the following faces:

1	2	3	1	2	3

Label the second cube with the following faces:

N	S	E	W	Roll	Roll

Label the third cube with the following faces:

NE	NW	SE	SW	NE	SW

Object
To be the first player to get 50 points or more

To Start
Place both disks on the box marked "Start Here." Choose the starting player by rolling the die. The player with the higher number goes first.

Rules
1. The starting player rolls the cube with "N,S, E, W, Roll, Roll" on it. If it shows a direction on top, he or she then rolls the number cube to see how far to go in that direction. For example, if the player rolls N and 2, he or she would move two spaces North and land on 5. The player would get 5 points.
2. If the cube thrown shows "Roll" on top, the player rolls the other cube for a new direction. He or she then rolls the number cube for the number of moves.
3. If a player cannot make the move thrown, the turn is lost (for example, N 3, because North can only go two spaces).
4. After figuring the total, the player returns to the "Start Here" box.
5. Players alternate turns and always begin at the "Start Here" box. The first player to get 50 or more points wins.

Place Value Roll

90	9
80	8
70	7
60	6
50	5
40	4
30	3
20	2
10	1

Place Value Roll

Players

Two players

Materials

2 red disks, 2 blue disks, and a pair of dice

Object

To be the first player to reach 99 or more

To Start

Choose the starting player by rolling the dice. The player with the higher number goes first.

Rules

1. The starting player rolls the dice and adds the top faces. That number is covered on the board, for example:

   7 is covered on the board.

2. The next player rolls the dice and does the same thing.
3. On the starting player's second turn, he or she rolls the dice and adds that total to the sum rolled on the first turn. To score totals greater than 10, the player will need to use two disks. For example, to show 36 on the board, the player places one disk on 30 and one disk on 6.
4. Players alternate turns until one player reaches 99 or more.

Making "15"

Making "15"

Players

Two players

Materials

4 red disks, 4 blue disks, and 1 die

Object

To be the first player to get exactly 15 points with the sum of any three of his or her four disks

To Start

Choose the starting player by rolling the die. The player with the higher number goes first.

Rules

1. The starting player puts a disk on any number. Then the next player puts a disk on any uncovered number.
2. Players alternate turns.
3. A player may move any one of his or her four disks to *any* unoccupied space.
4. The first player to get exactly 15 points with any three of his or her four disks wins.

Change for a Dollar

	1¢	5¢	10¢	25¢	50¢
◯	◯	◯	◯	◯	◯
◯	◯	◯	◯	◯	◯
◯	◯	◯	◯	◯	◯
◯	◯	◯	◯	◯	◯
◯	◯	◯	◯	◯	◯

© Addison-Wesley Publishing Company

Change for a Dollar

Players
Two players

Materials
15 red disks, 15 blue disks, 1 die, and 2 cubes
Label one cube with the following faces:

5	5	7	8	9	0

Label the second cube with the following faces:

20	30	40	50	60	70

Object
To have the most money when the game ends

To Start
Choose the starting player by rolling the die. The player with the higher number goes first.

Rules
1. The starting player rolls the two cubes and forms a money sum with that roll. The player then subtracts that sum from $1.00 and covers the answer on the board. For example:

20	8

   = 28¢ $1.00 − 28¢ = 72¢

   The player can cover any number of coins that equal 72¢.
2. Players alternate turns until a player cannot cover all his or her answer on the board.
3. The player with the most money covered wins.

Dice Combo

1,1	1,2	1,3	1,4	1,5	1,6
2,1	2,2	2,3	2,4	2,5	2,6
3,1	3,2	3,3	3,4	3,5	3,6
4,1	4,2	4,3	4,4	4,5	4,6
5,1	5,2	5,3	5,4	5,5	5,6
6,1	6,2	6,3	6,4	6,5	6,6

Dice Combo

Players

Two players

Materials

13 red disks, 13 blue disks, and a pair of dice

Object

To be the first player to reach exactly 100 points

To Start

Choose the starting player by rolling the dice. The player with the higher number goes first.

Rules

1. The starting player throws the dice and covers the numbers rolled on the playing board. For example, a roll of

   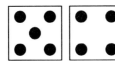

   would allow the player to cover either 4,5 or 5,4.
2. To score, the player adds, subtracts, multiplies, or divides the numbers rolled. In the example above, the score could be 9 (5 + 4), 1 (5 − 4), or 20 (5 × 4). (Only whole numbers may be scored.)
3. A player cannot cover a disk that has been played.
4. Play continues until one player reaches exactly 100. (A player cannot go over 100 and then subtract.)
5. If a player does not use the numbers rolled for his or her total, then a space should not be covered on the board.

Binary "200"

A [ ] 1

B [ ] 2

C [ ] 4

D [ ] 8

E [ ] 16

Binary "200"

Players
Two players

Materials
5 red disks, 5 blue disks, and 1 die

Object
To be the first player to total 200 points or more

To Start
Choose the starting player by rolling the die. The player with the higher number goes first.

Rules
1. Each player will throw the die a total of five times during a turn, filling each of the five boxes with a disk.
2. The starting player throws the die. If the roll is an odd number, he or she places a *red* disk in Box A. If the roll is an even number, he or she places a *blue* disk in Box A. The player throws the die for each of the other boxes (B, C, D, and E), placing a red disk for an odd number and a blue disk for an even number.
3. At the end of each turn, the player totals his or her score as follows: Red disks are worth 0 points. Blue disks are worth the number shown below the box.
4. After each turn, the player clears the boxes of disks.
5. The first player to total 200 points or more wins.

Cube Remainder

8	16	24	32	40
7	15	23	31	39
6	14	22	30	38
5	13	21	29	37
4	12	20	28	36
3	11	19	27	35
2	10	18	26	34
1	9	17	25	33

Cube Remainder

Players
Two players

Materials
40 disks of any color, 1 die, and 1 cube with its 6 faces marked:
5, 7, 9, 11, 12, and 13

Object
To have the most disks when the game ends

To Start
1. Choose the starting player by rolling the die. The player with the higher number goes first.
2. Cover all 40 circles with disks.

Rules
1. The starting player throws the numbered cube and divides the number rolled into the number of disks on the board. The player gives the *opponent* the number of disks representing the remainder. For example:

$$\boxed{11} \qquad 11\overline{)40}\ \ \overset{3}{}\ \text{R}7$$

Opponent takes 7 disks starting at circle 40.

2. The second player does the same, except he or she divides the number rolled into the number of disks left on the board. For example:

$$\boxed{5} \qquad 5\overline{)33}\ \overset{6}{}\ \text{R}3$$

Opponent takes 3 disks starting at circle 33.

3. The game continues until the board is empty. For example, if there are 7 disks left on the board, the last play might be:

$$\boxed{12} \qquad 12\overline{)7}\ \overset{0}{}\ \text{R}7$$

4. The player with the most disks wins.

Remainder Bingo

7	16	22	36	26
21	33	64	56	48
38	27	71	11	39
19	15	28	32	30
55	14	29	57	31

Remainder Bingo

Players

Two players

Materials

13 red disks, 13 blue disks, and a pair of dice

Object

To get four disks in a row—horizontally, vertically, or diagonally

To Start

Choose the starting player by rolling the dice. The player with the higher number goes first.

Rules

1. The starting player throws the dice and forms a division problem using the numbers rolled. The smaller number is the remainder and the larger number is the divisor. For example:

       $5\overline{)\ ?\ }\ R2$

2. The player then tries to find a number on the playing board that could represent the dividend in a division problem using those numbers and covers that number with a disk. In the example above, numbers 7, 27, 32, or 57 could be covered.

3. If both numbers rolled are the same, then consider the remainder to be 0. For example:

       $3\overline{)\ \ }\ R0$

    Numbers 36, 21, 48, 27, 39, 15, 30, or 57 could be covered.

4. If a number is covered, it cannot be used again.

5. The game can end when no one could possibly get four disks in a row. Then the player with the most rows of three disks wins.

Shape Bingo

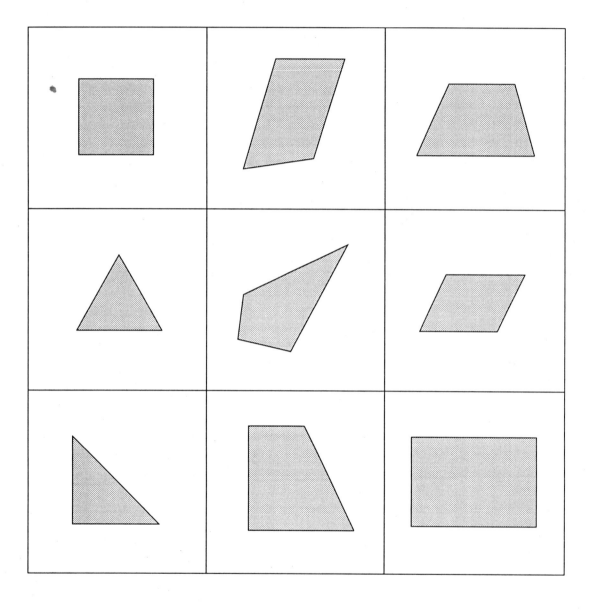

Shape Bingo

Players
Two players

Materials
5 red disks, 5 blue disks, 1 die, and 2 cubes
Label one cube with the following faces:

rectangle	triangle	four sides	three sides	polygon	quadri- lateral

Label the second cube with the following faces:

no 45-degree angle	a 45-degree angle	a right angle	no right angle	parallel lines	no parallel lines

Object
To get three disks in a row—horizontally, vertically, or diagonally

To Start
Choose the starting player by rolling the die. The player with the higher number goes first.

Rules
1. The starting player rolls both cubes and covers with a disk any shape that matches the information on the two top faces of the cubes. If a player cannot find a figure that matches, he or she loses a turn.
2. Players alternate turns.
3. The first player to get three disks in a row wins.

Variation: Use cutout shapes of your own creation on a blank 3 x 3 or 4 x 4 grid.

Making Squares

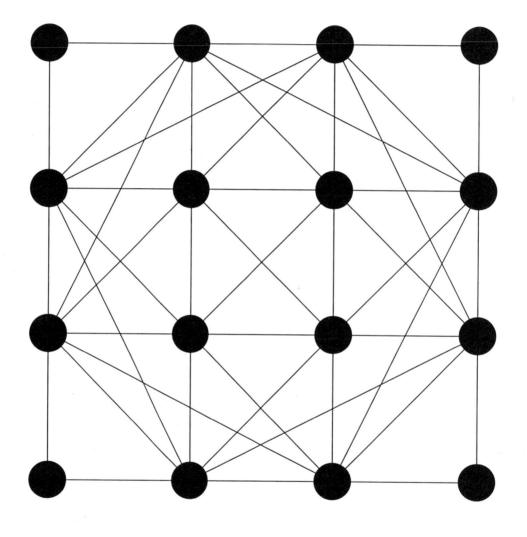

Making Squares

Players

Two players

Materials

8 red disks, 8 blue disks, and 1 die

Object

To make a square with four disks

To Start

Choose the starting player by rolling the die. The player with the higher number goes first.

Rules

1. A player covers any black dot on a turn.
2. Players alternate turns.
3. The game ends when the first player identifies four of his or her disks that form a square.
4. The sides of the square don't have to be vertical and horizontal. The four disks shown below form a square:

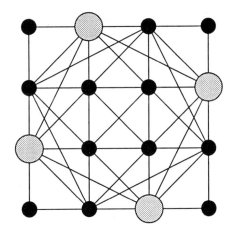

Note: The game may end in a tie.

Time on My Hands

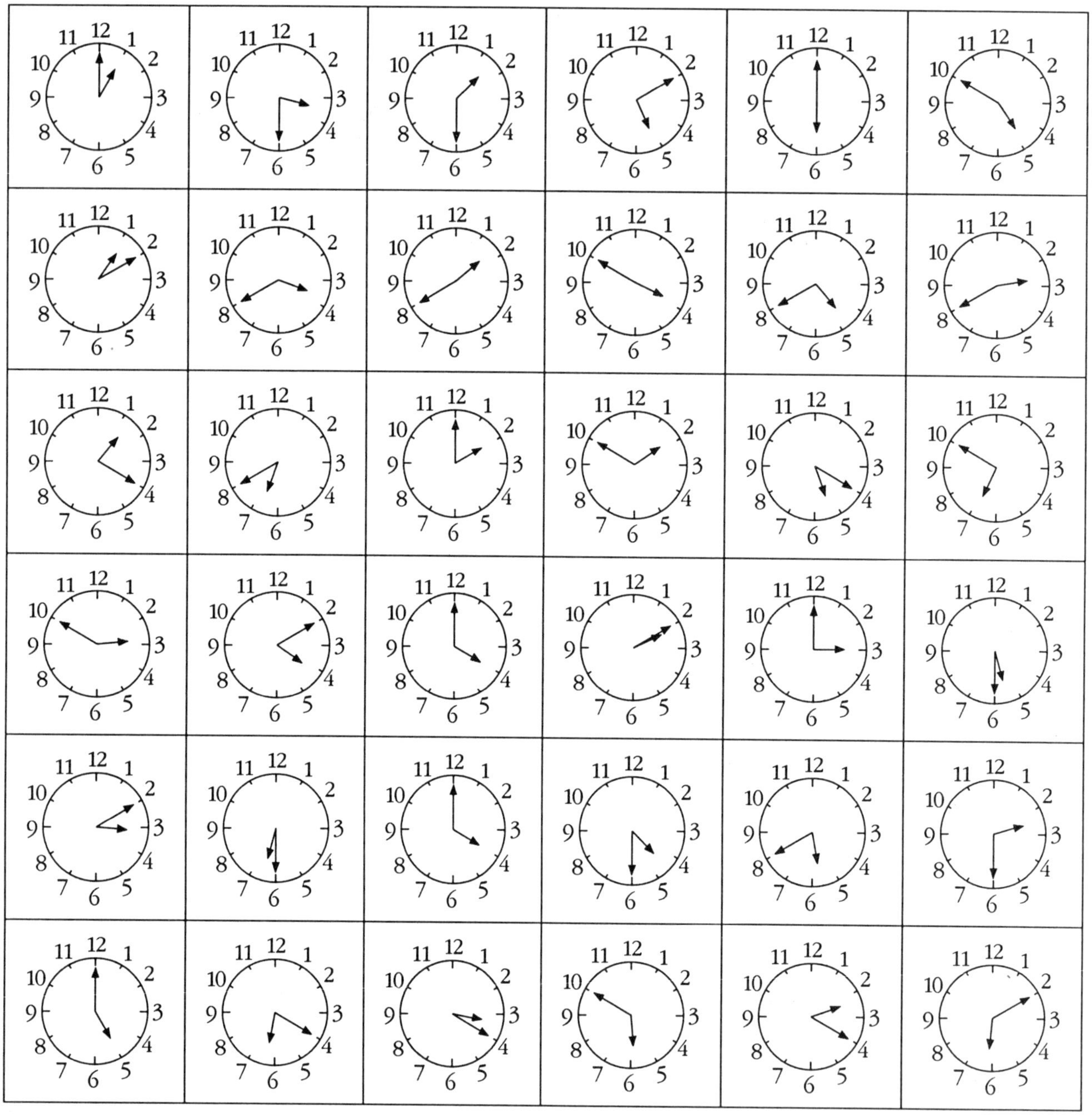

 © Addison-Wesley Publishing Company

Time on My Hands

Players

Two players

Materials

15 red disks, 15 blue disks, 1 die, and 2 cubes
Label one cube with the following faces:

hour 1:00	hour 2:00	hour 3:00	hour 4:00	hour 5:00	hour 6:00

Label the second cube with the following faces:

mins. :00	mins. :10	mins. :20	mins. :30	mins. :40	mins. :50

Object

To be the first player to get three disks in a row—vertically, horizontally, or diagonally

To Start

Choose the starting player by rolling the die. The player with the higher number goes first.

Rules

1. The starting player rolls both cubes to determine the time on the cube faces. The player then covers the clock face on the board with that time.
2. Players alternate turns.
3. If a clock face is already covered, the player loses that turn.
4. The first player to get three disks in a row wins.

Meter Math

Meter	100 Kilometers	Kilometer
Decameter	Decimeter	Millimeter
Hectometer	10 Kilometers	Centimeter

Meter Math

Players
Two players

Materials
5 red disks, 5 blue disks, 1 die, and 2 cubes
Label one cube with the following faces:

10	100	1000	$\dfrac{1}{10}$	$\dfrac{1}{100}$	$\dfrac{1}{1000}$

Label the second cube with the following faces:

m	dm	cm	km	mm	dkm

Object
To get three disks in a row—vertically, horizontally, or diagonally

To Start
Choose the starting player by rolling the die. The player with the higher number goes first.

Rules
1. The starting player throws both cubes and uses the roll to match an equivalent metric measure on the playing board. For example:

   | 10 | dm | = 1 meter (cover the "meter" square)
   |----|----|

2. Players alternate turns.
3. If a player forms a measure already covered on the board, he or she can remove the opponent's disk and replace it with his or her disk.
4. The first player to get three disks in a row wins.

Three-in-a-Row

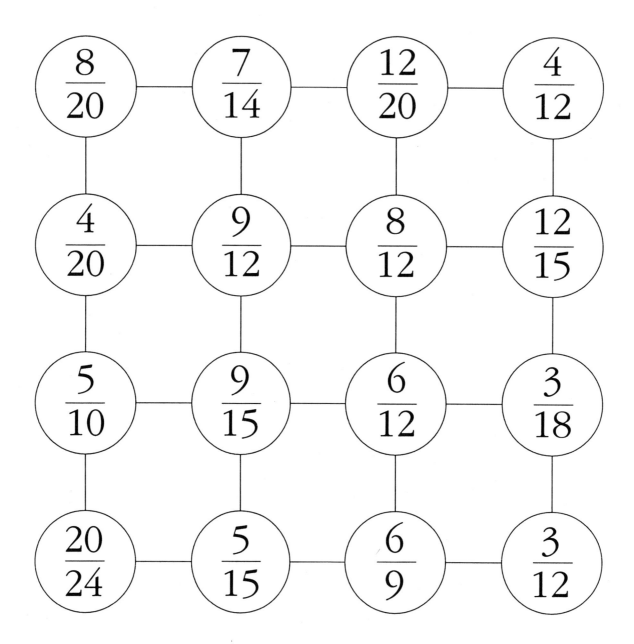

$$\frac{8}{20} \qquad \frac{7}{14} \qquad \frac{12}{20} \qquad \frac{4}{12}$$

$$\frac{4}{20} \qquad \frac{9}{12} \qquad \frac{8}{12} \qquad \frac{12}{15}$$

$$\frac{5}{10} \qquad \frac{9}{15} \qquad \frac{6}{12} \qquad \frac{3}{18}$$

$$\frac{20}{24} \qquad \frac{5}{15} \qquad \frac{6}{9} \qquad \frac{3}{12}$$

Three-in-a-Row

Players
Two players

Materials
8 red disks, 8 blue disks, and a pair of dice

Object
To get three disks in a row—vertically, horizontally, or diagonally

To Start
Choose the starting player by rolling the dice. The player with the higher number goes first.

Rules
1. On a turn, a player throws the dice and makes a proper fraction with the numbers rolled. The player then finds an equivalent fraction on the board and covers it with a disk. For example:

   Roll $\boxed{6}\boxed{2}$ $= \frac{2}{6} \rightarrow$ cover $\frac{4}{12}$

2. If an opponent's disk is already there, it may be removed.
3. If a player rolls doubles, he or she loses a turn.
4. The first player to get three disks in a row wins.

Percent Lineup

50%	125%	$33\frac{1}{3}\%$	200%
$83\frac{1}{3}\%$	40%	25%	300%
20%	100%	75%	$66\frac{2}{3}\%$
60%	$16\frac{2}{3}\%$	80%	250%

Percent Lineup

Players
Two players

Materials
9 red disks, 9 blue disks, and a pair of dice

Object
To get three disks in a row—vertically, horizontally, or diagonally

To Start
Choose the starting player by rolling the dice. The player with the higher number goes first.

Rules
1. The starting player rolls the dice and forms a fraction from the numbers rolled. The player then calculates the equivalent percent, for example:

   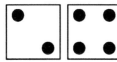 $\frac{2}{4}$ = 50%, or $\frac{4}{2}$ = 200%

   The player then covers one of the calculated percents on the board.
2. Players alternate turns.
3. A player may remove an opponent's disk if he or she rolls that percent.
4. The first player to get three in a row wins.

Fraction Race

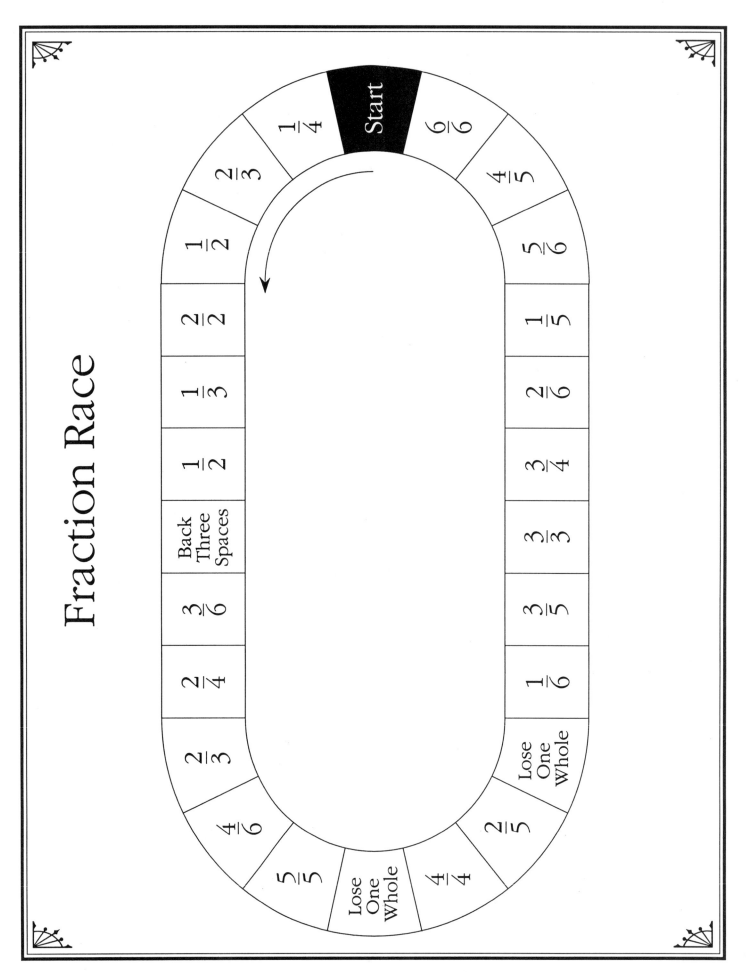

Fraction Race

Players

Two players

Materials

1 red disk, 1 blue disk, and 2 pairs of dice

Object

To be the first player to total 7 or more

To Start

Each player puts a marker on the "Start" position.

Rules

1. Simultaneously, each player rolls a pair of dice. Each player forms a fraction using the smaller number as the numerator and the larger as the denominator.

2. Players compare fractions. The player with the larger fraction moves his or her disk the number of moves in the denominator of the fraction. For example:

Player one has $\frac{3}{5}$.   Player two has $\frac{2}{4}$.

Since $\frac{3}{5}$ is larger than $\frac{2}{4}$, player one moves 5 spaces (the denominator number).

Players score the amount of the fraction in the space they move to.
Only the player who moves scores during that turn.

3. The game continues around the track, and players keep a running total of their scores.

4. The first player to total 7 or more wins.

Decimal Ring

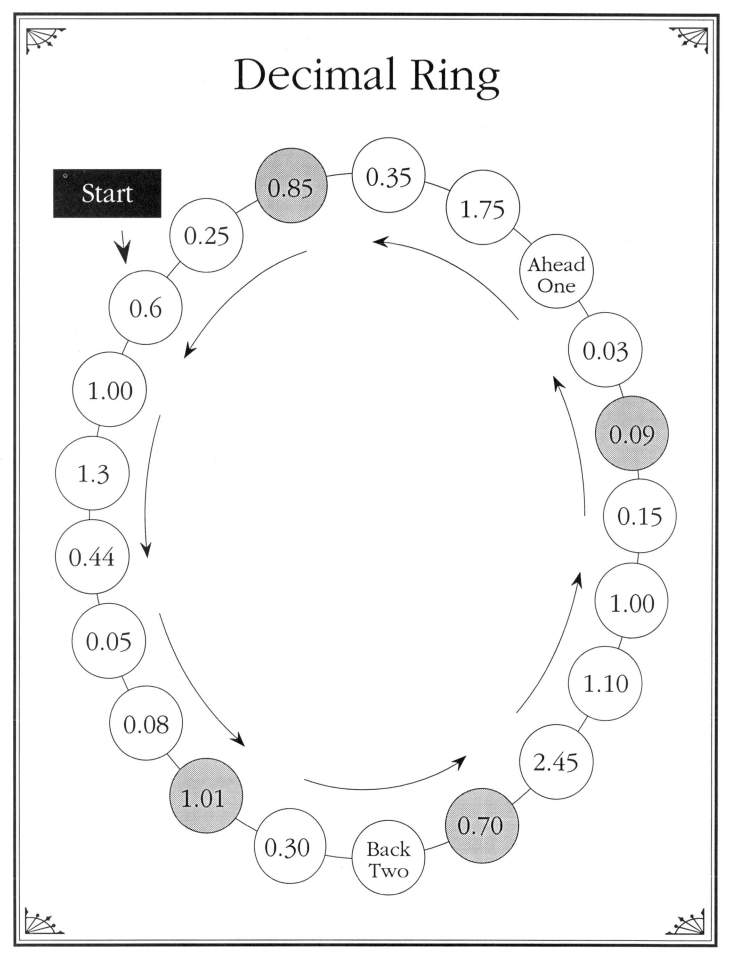

Decimal Ring

Players
Two players

Materials
1 red disk, 1 blue disk, and 1 die

Object
To be the first player to total 7.00 or more

To Start
Choose the starting player by rolling the die. The player with the higher number goes first.

Rules
1. The starting player places his or her disk on "Start," rolls the die, and moves the number of circles indicated on the die. The player's score for that turn is the decimal in the circle landed upon.
2. Players alternate turns, keeping a running total of their decimal scores.
3. If a player lands on a shaded circle, he or she subtracts that number from the total.
4. The first player to total 7.00 or more wins.

Following Directions

Go back three spaces unless you rolled a prime.	Advance two spaces if you rolled a multiple of 3.	**End**
Divisible by 2 and 3, stay. Others back one space.	5 only, or back one space.	
Go back five spaces unless you rolled a 1 or a 6.	All can stay.	
Advance one space if you rolled a factor of 18.	Multiple of 2, or back one space.	
Least common multiple of 2 and 3, advance two spaces.	Lowest common divisor of 9 and 12, advance three spaces.	
Square numbers can stay. Others go back two spaces.	Even numbers only, or back two spaces.	

Greater than 3, or back one space.		Go back two spaces.
All can stay.		
Go back to Start unless you rolled an odd number.		
Go back one space unless you rolled a number less than 3.		
If you didn't roll an even number, go back one space.	**Start**	
Not prime? Then go back to Start.		

Following Directions

Players
Two players

Materials
1 red disk, 1 blue disk, and 1 die

Object
To be the first player to complete the board

To Start
1. Choose the starting player by rolling the die. The player with the higher number goes first.
2. Each player places his or her disk on the start position.

Rules
1. The starting player rolls the die and moves the number of spaces rolled.
2. The player follows the directions in the space, based on the number he or she rolled.
3. Players alternate turns.
4. The player who reaches "End" first wins.

Factor Roll

5	3	7	Prime
2	6	8	17
Prime	21	4	16
13	9	Prime	26

Factor Roll

Players

Two players

Materials

10 red disks, 10 blue disks, and a pair of dice

Object

To get four disks in a row—horizontally, vertically, or diagonally

To Start

Choose the starting player by rolling the dice. The player with the higher number goes first.

Rules

1. The starting player rolls the dice and forms a two-digit number with the numbers rolled. The larger number represents tens, and the smaller represents units. For example:

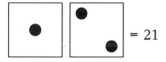 = 21

2. The player then puts a disk on any number (only one) on the playing board that is a factor of that number. For example, 21 can cover 3, 7, or 21.
3. If a player rolls a double (11, 22, 33, etc.), the turn is lost.
4. If a player rolls a PRIME, he or she can place a disk on any "Prime" square.
5. If a square is already occupied, a player cannot use it.
6. Players alternate turns.
7. The first player to get four disks in a row wins.
8. If players get to a point where no one can possibly win, they start a new game.

Fill the "A"

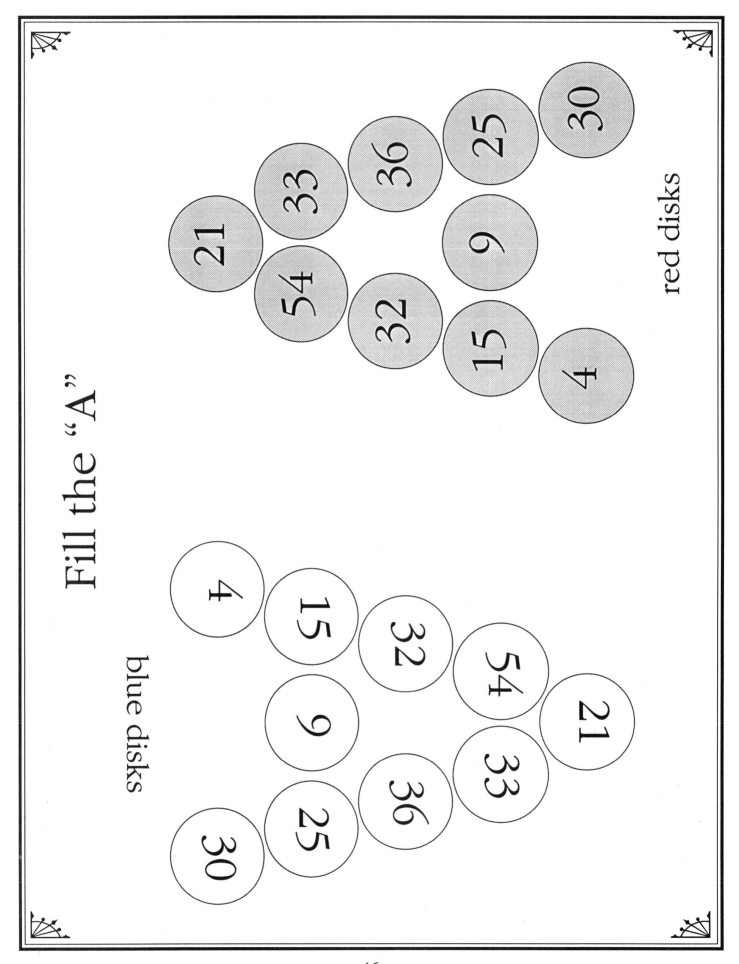

red disks

blue disks

Fill the "A"

Players
Two players

Materials
10 red disks, 10 blue disks, and 1 die

Object
To be the first player to fill his or her playing board

To Start
Choose the starting player by rolling the die. The player with the higher number goes first.

Rules
1. The first player rolls the die and covers any number on his or her playing board that is a multiple of the number on the die. For example, if the red-disk player rolls 5, he or she covers 15, 25, or 30.
2. Players alternate turns.
3. If a 1 is rolled, the player loses his or her turn.
4. The first player to fill his or her playing board wins.

Prime Snake

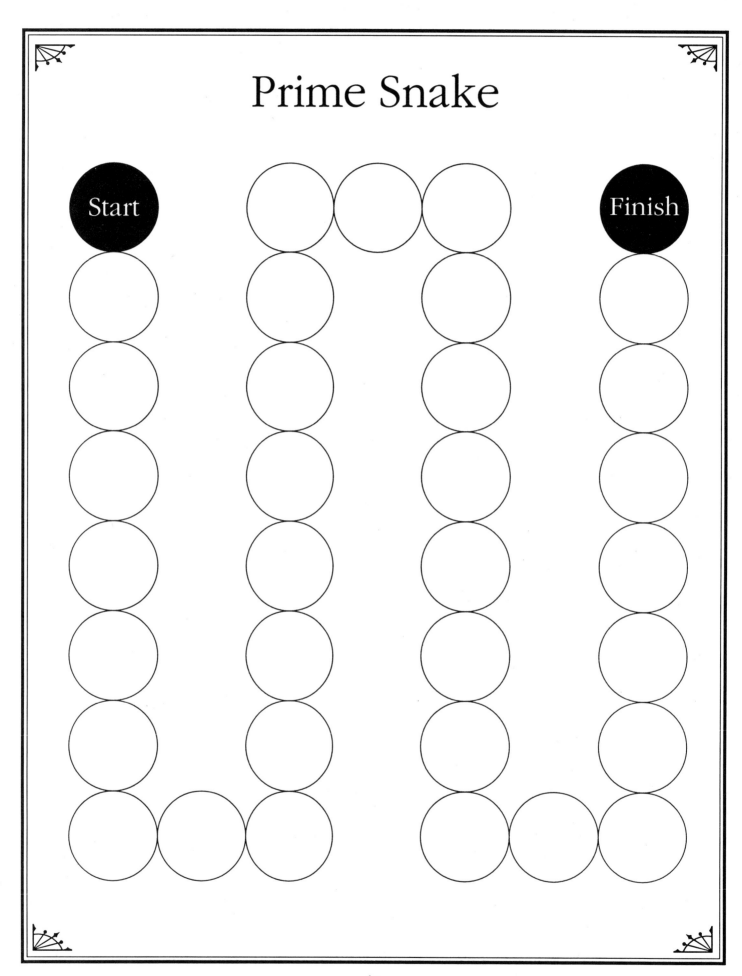

Prime Snake

Players

Two players

Materials

1 red disk, 1 blue disk, and a pair of dice

Object

To cross "Finish" first

To Start

Choose the starting player by rolling the dice. The player with the higher number is "Prime" and goes first.

Rules

1. If the "Prime" player rolls a prime number (2, 3, 5, 7, or 11), he or she moves the number of 2s in that number. For example, on a roll of 7, the player could move three spaces, since there are three 2s in 7. If a composite number is rolled, the "Prime" player cannot move.
2. The "Composite" player must roll a composite number less than 12, that is, 4, 6, 8, 9, or 10. The player then moves the number of 2s in his or her roll.
3. If a 12 is rolled by either player, he or she loses a turn.
4. The first player to cross "Finish" wins.

Cover All

Player A				Player B

Cover All

Players
Two players

Materials
11 red disks, 11 blue disks, 1 die, and 1 cube
Label one cube with the following faces:

1	2	3	1	2	3

Object
To be the first player to cover the board completely with his or her disks

To Start
Choose the starting player by rolling the die. The player with the higher number goes first.

Rules
1. The starting player rolls the cube and begins at "Player A" placing the number of disks in order, one to a block, as indicated on the top face of the cube.
2. The second player begins at "Player B," rolls the cube, and fills in the blocks.
3. Players alternate turns. If any of the opponent's disks are in the way, the player removes them.
4. The first player to completely cover the board wins.

Number Signs

8	1	0	2
3	7	6	5
4	9	5	4
12	7	10	3

Number Signs

Players

Two players

Materials

10 red disks, 10 blue disks, 1 die, and 1 cube
Label the cube with the following faces:

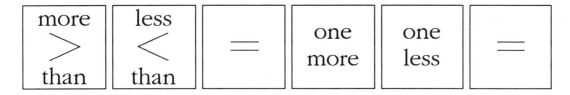

Object

To get three disks in a row—vertically, horizontally, or diagonally

To Start

Choose the starting player by rolling the die. The player with the higher number goes first.

Rules

1. The starting player rolls the cube and the die and covers a number on the board that corresponds to the roll of the die and the cube. For example, if a player rolls

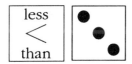

he or she can cover any number that is less than 3.
2. Only one number can be covered on a turn.
3. Players alternate turns.
4. The first player to get three disks in a row wins.

Capture

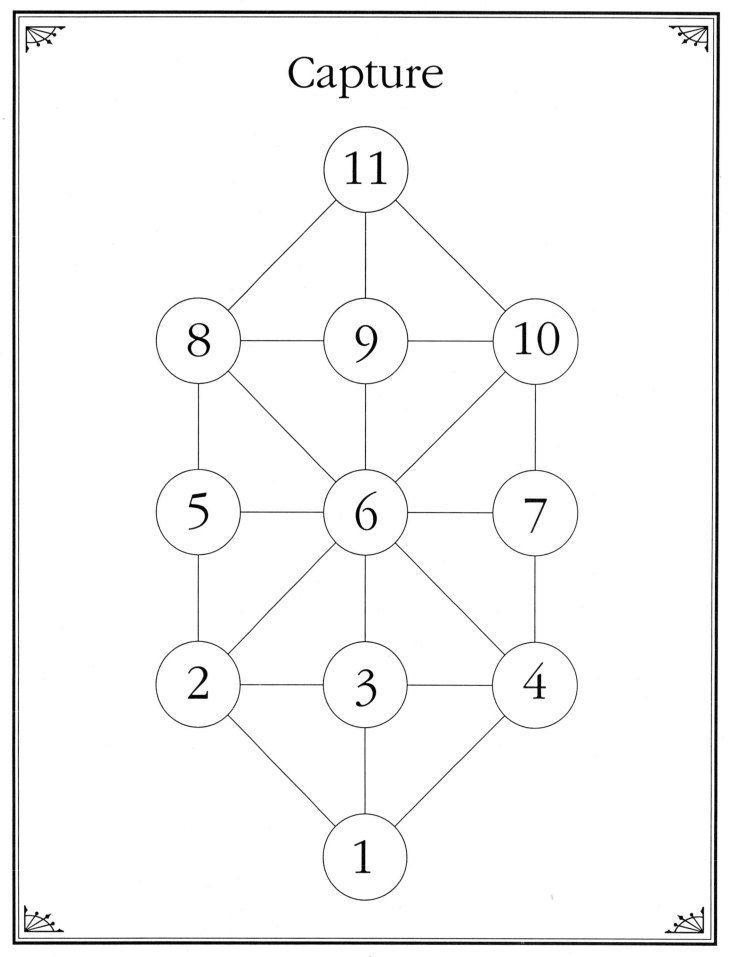

Capture

Players
Two players

Materials
3 red disks, 1 blue disk, and 1 die

Object
The spy wins if he or she occupies space 1. The agents win if they trap the spy in space 11.

To Start
Choose the starting player by rolling the die. The player with the higher number goes first.

Rules
1. The starting player chooses to be either the spy or the agents. The spy (blue disk) starts on any unoccupied space except space 3. The agents (red disks) start on spaces 1, 2, and 4.
2. The agents move first.
3. Players alternate turns moving one disk on a turn to any vacant space that is connected by a line.
4. The agents can move only left, right, and up (no backwards moves). The spy can move in any direction.
5. The agents win if they trap the spy in space 11 and occupy spaces 8, 9, and 10. The spy wins by getting to space 1.
6. No jumping is allowed.

Two-Player Shift

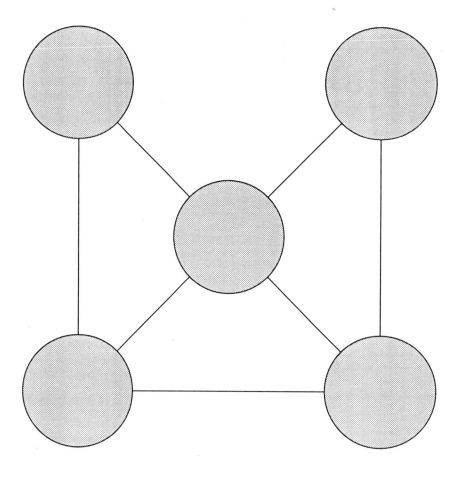

Two-Player Shift

Players
Two players

Materials
2 red disks, 2 blue disks, and 1 die

Object
To block an opponent so he or she cannot move

To Start
Choose the starting player by rolling the die. The player with the higher number goes first.

Rules
1. The starting player first places his or her two disks on the playing board. Then the second player places his or her two disks on the board.
2. Players alternate turns by sliding one of their two disks along a line to an empty space.
3. No jumping or removing is allowed.
4. The first player who cannot move loses.

Alternate

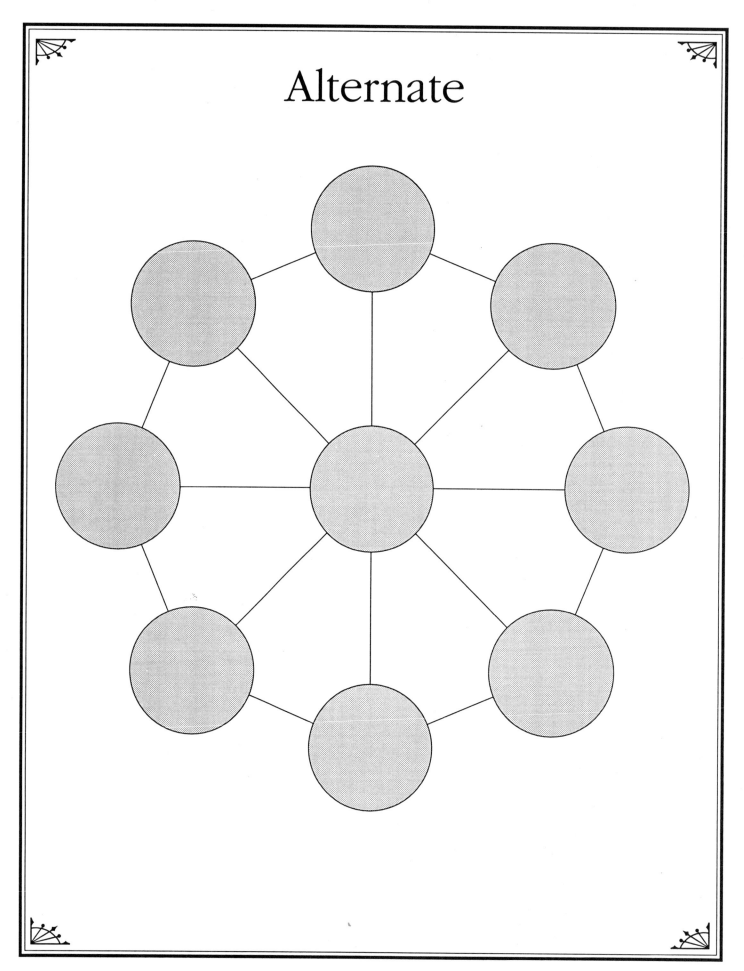

Alternate

Players
Two players

Materials
4 red disks, 4 blue disks, and 1 die

Object
To block an opponent so that he or she cannot move

To Start
1. Place the disks alternately on the outside eight circles (red, blue, red, blue, red, etc.).
2. Choose the starting player by rolling the die. The player with the higher number goes first.

Rules
1. Players alternate turns moving one of his or her disks from one circle to a vacant circle connected by a straight line.
2. A player cannot jump a disk or occupy a circle that is already covered.
3. The first player who cannot make a move loses.

Remove It

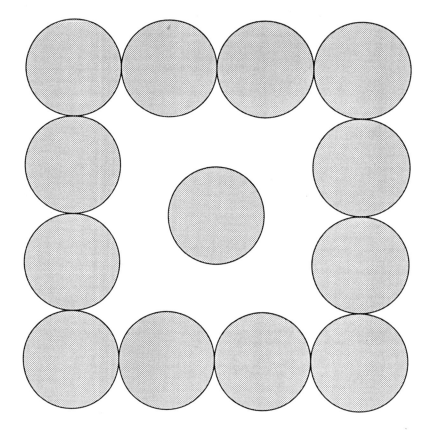

Remove It

Players

Two players

Materials

13 disks and 1 die

Object

To be the player to remove the last disk

To Start

1. Place a disk on each of the 13 circles.
2. Choose the starting player by rolling the die. The player with the higher number goes first.

Rules

1. The starting player can remove either one disk or two disks (if they are in touching circles).
2. Players alternate turns.
3. The player who removes the last disk wins.

Disk Switch

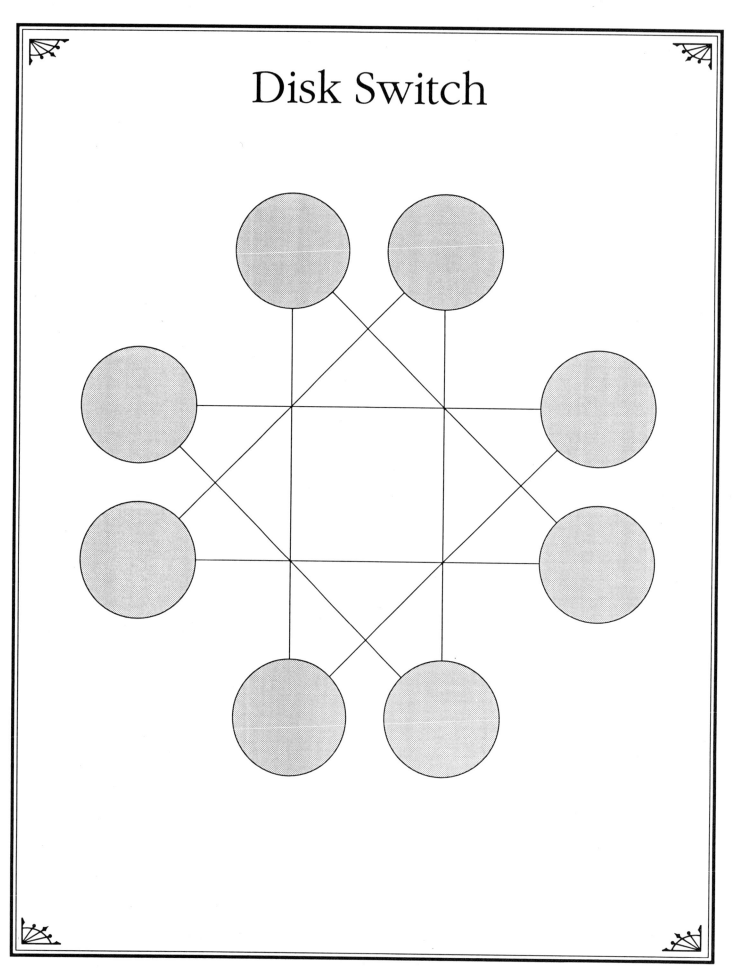

Disk Switch

Players
One player

Materials
7 disks

Object
To place all seven disks on the playing board

Rules
1. Place a disk on any unoccupied dot and move it along one line segment to a different dot.
2. Next, place a second disk on any unoccupied dot and move it along the same way.
3. Once a disk is placed, it cannot be moved again.
4. Continue placing the disks as described above until all disks have been placed.

Divide a Dozen

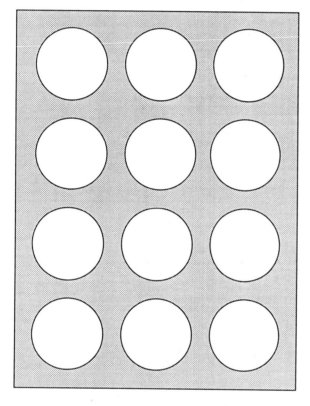

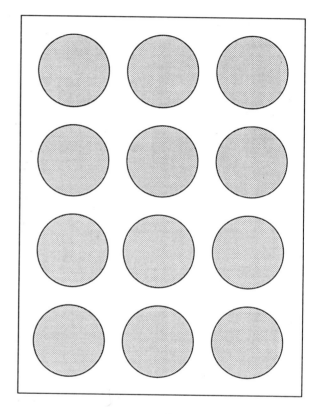

Left

Right

Divide a Dozen

Players

Two players

Materials

12 disks of one color and 1 die

Object

To remove the last single disk

To Start

1. Choose the starting player by rolling the die. The player with the higher number goes first.
2. The first player divides the 12 disks into two uneven piles. He or she then places one pile of disks in the circles on the left and the other pile in the circles on the right.

Rules

1. On a player's turn, he or she removes as many disks as he or she wants from one box, OR the player can remove an equal number from each box.
2. Players alternate turns until one player removes the last single disk. That player is the winner.

Five-Up

red	blue	red	blue	red
blue	red	blue	red	blue

Five-Up

Players

Two players

Materials

5 red disks, 5 blue disks, and 1 die

Object

To get five disks in a row—vertically, horizontally, or diagonally

To Start

1. Choose the starting player by rolling the die. The player with the higher number goes first.
2. Place alternating red and blue disks in the top and bottom rows of the board.

Rules

1. Players may move one square at a time, in any direction—vertically, horizontally, or diagonally.
2. Players cannot jump any disk.
3. The first player to get five of his or her disks in a row wins.

Blocked

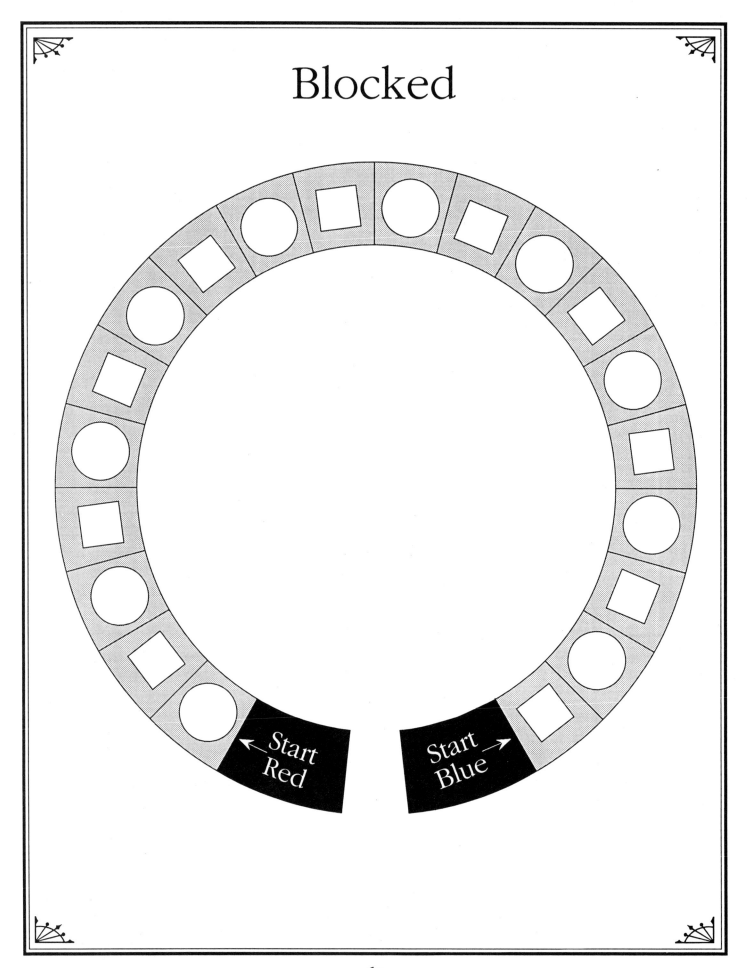

Start Red

Start Blue

Blocked

Players

Two players

Materials

1 red disk, 1 blue disk, and a pair of dice

Object

To be the player on a circle when the two disks meet

To Start

1. Choose the starting player by throwing the dice. The player with the higher number goes first.
2. Place the red and blue disks on their starting positions.

Rules

1. Each player must move his or her disk 1, 2, or 3 spaces during a turn.
2. One disk cannot jump over another disk.
3. When the disks meet, the game is over.

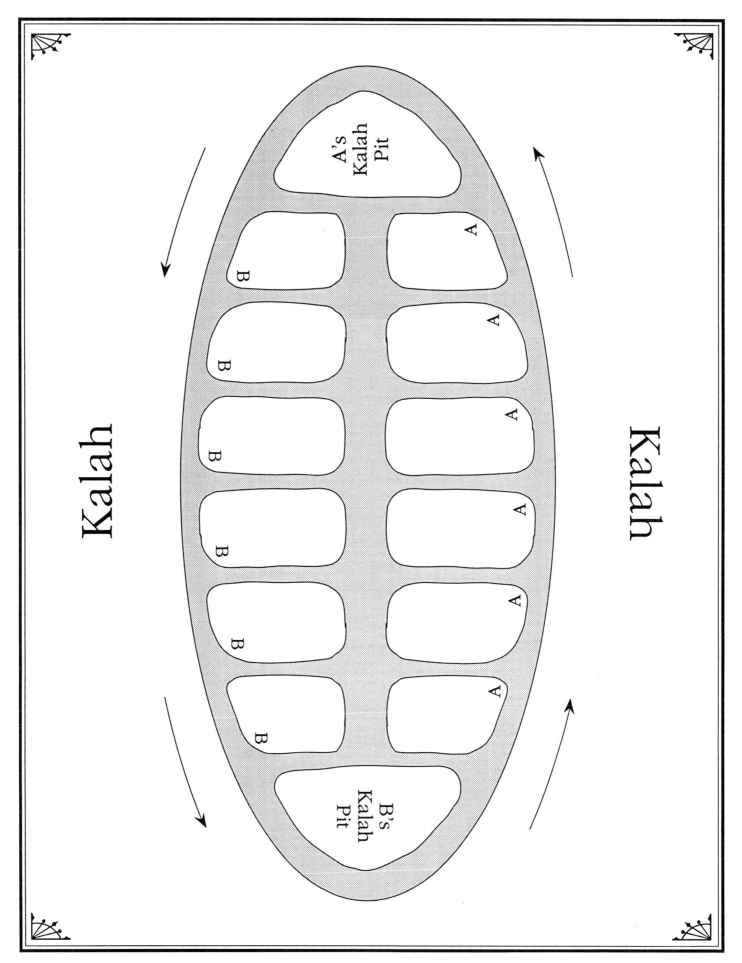

Kalah

Kalah

Kalah

Players
Two players

Materials
36 disks and 1 die

Object
To be the player with the most disks in his or her Kalah pit at the end of the game

To Start
1. Choose the starting player by rolling the die. The player with the higher number goes first.
2. Place three disks in each of the 12 A and B pits on the playing board.

Rules
1. The starting player chooses to be player A or player B. Each player owns six pits and a Kalah pit. As they face each other, each player's Kalah pit is at the right end of his or her six pits.
2. Play moves counterclockwise.
3. On each turn, a player removes all the disks from one of his or her pits and places them, one at a time, in each succeeding pit (including his or her own Kalah pit). A player never places a disk in his or her opponent's Kalah pit when moving on a turn.
4. A disk in a player's own Kalah pit scores one point. Once a disk is in a Kalah pit, it cannot be removed.
5. If the player's last disk on a turn is dropped in his or her Kalah pit, then that player gets an extra turn.
6. If, on a player's turn, the last disk falls into one of his or her empty pits, then the player can "capture" all the disks from the opponent's pit that is directly opposite. These disks, as well as the player's capturing disk, are placed in the player's Kalah pit.
7. The game ends when a player has no disks on his or her side. At that point, the player with disks remaining places those disks in his or her Kalah pit.
8. The player with the most disks in his or her Kalah pit wins.

Corner

Corner

Players
Two players

Materials
8 red disks, 8 blue disks, and 1 die

Object
To corner the opponent so that he or she cannot place a disk

To Start
1. Choose the starting player by rolling the die. The player with the higher number goes first.
2. Each player has eight disks of one color.

Rules
1. The starting player places one disk anyplace on the board.
2. On the second player's turn, he or she must place one disk in the same row or column as the previously placed disk.
3. Players alternate turns placing one disk as described above.
4. A player cannot place a disk in a square where a disk lies between that position and the last placed disk. For example:

(R) represents the last played disk. Blue can play in position 1, 3, 4, or 5, but not 2. A blue disk lies between 2 and the last played disk.

5. The game ends when a player cannot play. That player loses.

Jumping Disks

Jumping Disks

Players

One player

Materials

9 disks

Object

To remove all disks except one left in the center

To Start

Place the 9 disks on the playing board as shown below.

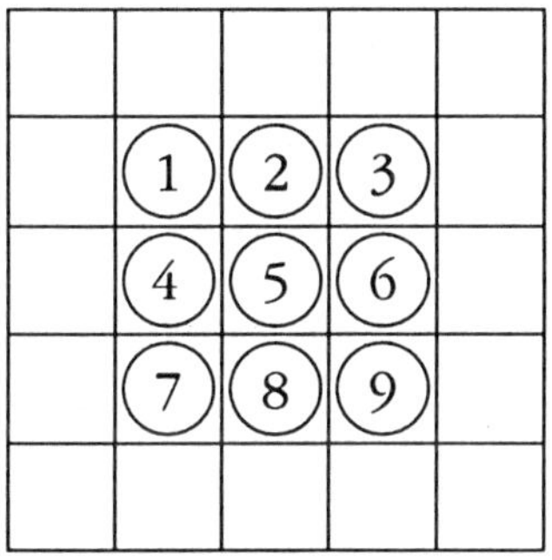

Rules

1. The player jumps over a disk, landing on an unoccupied space. The player removes the jumped piece as in the game of checkers.
2. Jumps are allowed horizontally, vertically, and diagonally.
3. It can be done so that there is one disk left in the center.

Reversi

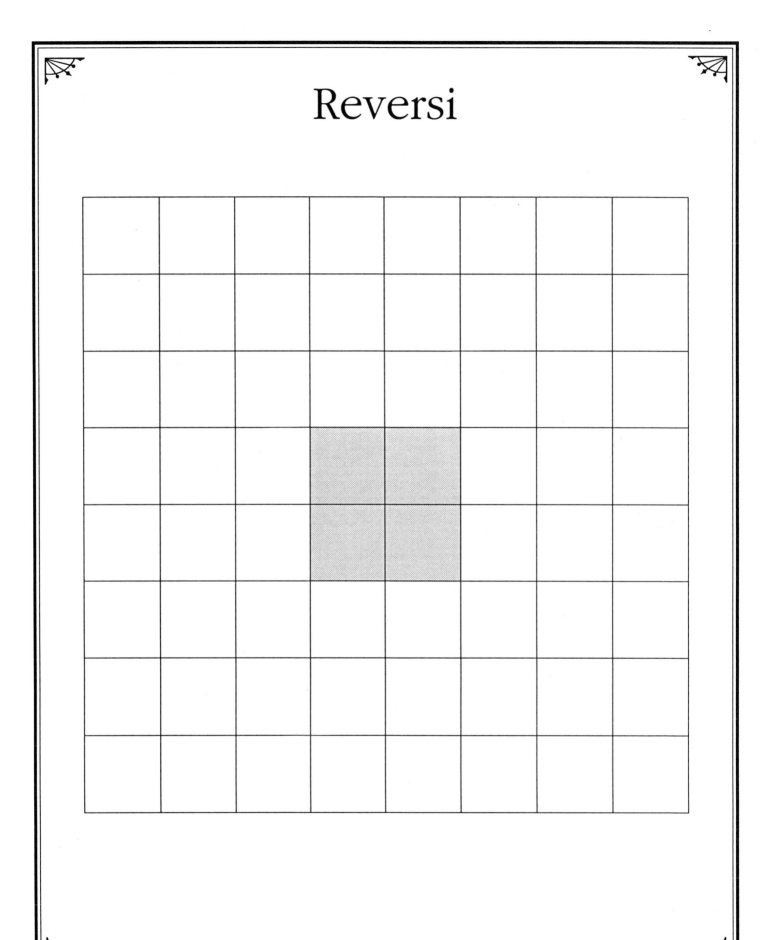

Reversi

Players
Two players

Materials
1 die and 40 disks with a color or design on one side and a different design on the other side. (Single-color disks can be adapted by placing a gummed label or dot on one side. Coins can also be used.)

Object
To be the player with the most disks on the board when the game ends

To Start
1. Choose the starting player by rolling the die. The player with the higher number goes first.
2. Place the first four disks in the center four squares on the board as shown.

Rules
1. The starting player chooses which side of the disks (design) will represent him or her.
2. A play must be made in a square that shares a vertex with a square covered by a different design disk.
3. The starting player places a disk to form a row that will have a disk of his or her design at each end. The row can be vertical, horizontal, or diagonal. The player then reverses to the opposite side the opponent's disk that is between his or her end disks. This disk now shows the first player's design.

4. The play described above is a "Reversi." If a player cannot create a "Reversi," then he or she loses the turn.

(continued)

5. Players alternate playing one disk at a time.
6. Disks once played on the board remain in that position, but they may be turned over many times during the game.
7. More than one row of disks can be "Reversied" by playing a single disk. For example:

8. The game ends when neither player can play.